PENGUIN CLASSICS

Nothing . . . Except My Geniu
The Wit and Wisdom of Oscar Wilde

Oscar Fingal O'Flahertie Wills Wilde was born in Dublin in 1854, his father an eminent eye-surgeon and his mother a nationalist poet who wrote under the pseudonym 'Speranza'. He went to Trinity College, Dublin, and then to Magdalen College, Oxford, where he began to propagandize the new Aesthetic (or 'Art for Art's Sake') Movement. Despite winning a first and the Newdigate Prize for Poetry, Wilde failed to obtain an Oxford fellowship, and was forced to earn a living by public lecturing and writing for periodicals. He published a largely unsuccessful volume of poems in 1881 and in the next year undertook a lecture tour of the United States in order to promote the D'Oyly Carte production of Gilbert and Sullivan's comic opera *Patience*. After his marriage to Constance Lloyd in 1884, he tried to establish himself as a writer, but with little initial success. However, his three volumes of short fiction, *The Happy Prince* (1888), *Lord Arthur Savile's Crime* (1891) and *A House of Pomegranates* (1891), together with his only novel, *The Picture of Dorian Gray* (1891), gradually won him a reputation, confirmed and enhanced by the phenomenal success of his society comedies – *Lady Windermere's Fan, A Woman of No Importance, An Ideal Husband* and *The Importance of Being Earnest*, all performed on the West End stage between 1892 and 1895.

Success, however, was short-lived. In 1891 Wilde had met and fallen extravagantly in love with Lord Alfred Douglas. In 1895, when his success as a dramatist was at its height, Wilde brought an unsuccessful libel action against Douglas's father, the Marquess of Queensberry. Wilde lost the case and two trials later was sentenced to two years' imprisonment for acts of gross indecency. As a result of this experience he wrote *The Ballad of Reading Gaol*. He was released from prison in 1897 and went into an immediate self-imposed exile on the Continent. He died in Paris in ignominy in 1900.

OSCAR WILDE

Nothing . . . Except My Genius

The Wit and Wisdom of Oscar Wilde

PENGUIN BOOKS

PENGUIN CLASSICS

Published by the Penguin Group
Penguin Books Ltd, 80 Strand, London WC2R 0RL, England
Penguin Group (USA) Inc., 375 Hudson Street, New York, New York 10014, USA
Penguin Group (Canada), 90 Eglinton Avenue East, Suite 700, Toronto, Ontario, Canada M4P 2Y3
(a division of Pearson Penguin Canada Inc.)
Penguin Ireland, 25 St Stephen's Green, Dublin 2, Ireland (a division of Penguin Books Ltd)
Penguin Group (Australia), 250 Camberwell Road, Camberwell, Victoria 3124, Australia
(a division of Pearson Australia Group Pty Ltd)
Penguin Books India Pvt Ltd, 11 Community Centre, Panchsheel Park, New Delhi – 110 017, India
Penguin Group (NZ), 67 Apollo Drive, Rosedale, North Shore 0632, New Zealand
(a division of Pearson New Zealand Ltd)
Penguin Books (South Africa) (Pty) Ltd, 24 Sturdee Avenue, Rosebank, Johannesburg 2196, South Africa

Penguin Books Ltd, Registered Offices: 80 Strand, London WC2R 0RL, England

www.penguin.com

This selection first published in Penguin Classics 2010
007

Chronology copyright © Ian Small, 2003

All rights reserved

Set in 11.25/14 pt Monotype Dante
Typeset by Palimpsest Book Production Limited, Grangemouth, Stirlingshire
Printed in England by Clays Ltd, St Ives plc

Except in the United States of America, this book is sold subject
to the condition that it shall not, by way of trade or otherwise, be lent,
re-sold, hired out, or otherwise circulated without the publisher's prior consent in any
form of binding or cover other than that in which it is published and without a similar
condition including this condition being imposed on the subsequent purchaser

ISBN: 978-0-141-19268-0

www.greenpenguin.co.uk

MIX
Paper from
responsible sources
FSC
www.fsc.org   FSC™ C018179

Penguin Books is committed to a sustainable
future for our business, our readers and our planet.
This book is made from Forest Stewardship
Council™ certified paper.

Chronology

1882 Lecture tour of North America, speaking on art, aesthetics and decoration. Revised edition of *Poems* published.

1883 His first play, *Vera; or, The Nihilists* performed in New York; it is not a success.

1884 Marries Constance Lloyd in London, honeymoon in Paris and Dieppe.

1885 Moves into 16 Tite Street, Chelsea. Cyril Wilde born.

1886 Vyvyan Wilde born. Meets Robert Ross, to become his life-long friend and, in 1897, his literary executor. Ross may have been Wilde's first homosexual lover.

1887 Becomes the editor of *Lady's World: A Magazine of Fashion and Society*, and changes its name to *Woman's World*. Publication of 'The Canterville Ghost' and 'Lord Arthur Savile's Crime'.

1888 *The Happy Prince and Other Tales* published; on the whole well-received.

1889 'Pen, Pencil and Poison' (on the forger and poisoner Thomas Griffiths Wainewright), 'The Decay of Lying' (a dialogue in praise of artifice over nature and art over morality), 'The Portrait of Mr W. H.' (on the supposed identity of the dedicatee of Shakespeare's sonnets) all published.

1890 *The Picture of Dorian Gray* published in the July number of *Lippincott's Monthly Magazine*; fierce debate between Wilde and hostile critics ensues. 'The True Function and Value of Criticism' (later revised and included in *Intentions* as 'The Critic as Artist') published.

1891 Wilde's first meeting with Lord Alfred Douglas ('Bosie'). *The Duchess of Padua* performed in New York. 'The Soul of Man Under Socialism' and 'Preface to Dorian Gray' published in February and March in the *Fortnightly Review*. The revised and extended edition of *The Picture of Dorian Gray* published by Ward, Lock and Company in April. *Intentions* (collection of critical essays), *Lord Arthur Savile's Crime and Other Stories* and *A House of Pomegranates* (fairy-tales) published.

1892 *Lady Windermere's Fan* performed at St James's Theatre, London (February to July).

1893 *Salomé* published in French. *A Woman of No Importance* performed at the Haymarket Theatre, London.

1894 *Salomé* published in English with illustrations by Aubrey Beardsley; Douglas is the dedicatee. *The Sphinx*, a poem with illustrations by Charles Ricketts, published.

1895 *An Ideal Husband* opens at the Haymarket Theatre in January; it is followed by the hugely successful *The Importance of Being Earnest* at St James's Theatre in February. On 28 February Wilde returns to his club, the Albemarle, to find a card from Douglas's father, the Marquess of Queensberry, accusing Wilde of 'posing as a somdomite' (sodomite). Wilde quickly takes out an action accusing Queensberry of criminal libel. In April Queensberry appears at the Old Bailey and is acquitted, following a successful plea of justification on the basis that Wilde was guilty of homosexual behaviour. Wilde is immediately arrested, after ignoring his friends' advice to flee the country. In May he is tried twice at the Old Bailey, and on 25 May sentenced to two years' imprisonment with hard labour for 'acts of gross indecency with another male person'. In July he is sent to Wandsworth Prison. In November he is declared bankrupt, and shortly afterwards transferred to Reading Gaol.

1896 Death of Wilde's mother, Lady Jane Francesca Wilde ('Speranza').

1897 Wilde writes the long letter to Douglas that would be later entitled 'De Profundis'. In May Wilde is released from prison, and sails for Dieppe by the night ferry. He never returns to Britain.

1898 *The Ballad of Reading Gaol* published under the pseudonym

C.3.3, Wilde's cell-number in Reading Gaol. Wilde moves to Paris in February. Constance Wilde (who had by now changed her name to Holland) dies.

1899 Willie (b. 1852), Wilde's elder brother, dies.

1900 In January Queensberry dies. By July Wilde himself is very ill with a blood infection. On 29 November he is received into the Roman Catholic Church, and dies on 30 November in the Hôtel d'Alsace in Paris.

1905 An abridged version of *De Profundis*, edited by Robert Ross, published.

1908 The *Collected Works*, edited by Robert Ross, are published.

Nothing . . . Except My Genius

If you ask nine-tenths of the British public what is the meaning of the word aesthetics, they will tell you it is the French for affectation or the German for a dado . . .

To know nothing about their great men is one of the necessary elements of English education.

And criticism – what place is that to have in our culture? Well, I think that the first duty of an art critic is to hold his tongue at all times, and upon all subjects: *C'est un grand avantage de n'avoir rien fait, mais il ne faut pas en abuser.*

Art can never have any other claim but her own perfection: it is for the critic to create for art the social aim, too, by teaching the people the spirit in which they are to approach all artistic work, the love they are to give it, the lesson they are to draw from it.

. . . beauty is the only thing that time cannot harm. Philosophies fall away like sand, and creeds follow one another like the withered leaves of autumn; but what is beautiful is a joy for all seasons and a possession for all eternity.

. . . the good we get from art is not what we learn from it; it is what we become through it.

We spend our days, each one of us, in looking for the secret of life. Well, the secret of life is in art.

Had I been treated differently by the newspapers in England and in this country, had I been commended and endorsed, for the first time in my life I should have doubted myself and my mission . . . What possible difference can it make to me what the *New York Herald* says? You go and look at the statue of the Venus de Milo and you know that it is an exquisitely beautiful creation. Would it change your opinion in the least if all the newspapers in the land should pronounce it a wretched caricature? Not at all. I know that I am right, that I have a mission to perform. I am indestructible!

The supreme object of life is to live. Few people live. It is true life only to realize one's own perfection, to make one's every dream a reality.

To me the life of the businessman who eats his breakfast early in the morning, catches a train for the city, stays there in the dingy, dusty atmosphere of the commercial world, and goes back to his house in the evening, and after supper to sleep, is worse than the life of the galley slave – his chains are golden instead of iron.

Bad art is a great deal worse than no art at all.

No better way is there to learn to love Nature than to understand Art. It dignifies every flower of the field. And, the boy who sees the thing of beauty which a bird on the wing becomes when transferred to wood or canvas will probably not throw the customary stone. What we want is something spiritual added to life. Nothing is so ignoble that Art cannot sanctify it.

I would rather have discovered Mrs [Lillie] Langtry than have discovered America.

In the evening I went to the Casino . . . There I found the miners and the female friends of the miners, and in one corner a pianist – sitting at a piano over which was this notice: 'Please don't shoot the pianist; he is doing his best.' I was struck with this recognition of the fact that bad art merits the penalty of death, and I felt that in this remote city, where the aesthetic applications of the revolver were clearly established in the case of music, my apostolic task would be much simplified, as indeed it was.

. . . nothing is worth doing except what the world says is impossible.

Today more than ever the artist and a love of the beautiful are needed to temper and counteract the sordid materialism of the age. In an age when science has undertaken to declaim against the soul and spiritual nature of man, and when commerce is ruining beautiful rivers and magnificent woodlands and the glorious skies in its greed for gain, the artist comes forward as a priest and prophet of nature to protest . . .

To make a good salad is to be a brilliant diplomatist – the problem is entirely the same in both cases. To know exactly how much oil one must put with one's vinegar.

Life is much too important a thing ever to talk seriously about it.

There is always more brass than brains in an aristocracy.

Good kings are the only dangerous enemies that modern democracy has.

I have always been of the opinion that consistency is the last refuge of the unimaginative . . .

. . . the British cook is a foolish woman, who should be turned, for her iniquities, into a pillar of that salt which she never knows how to use.

Of Shakespeare it may be said he was the first to see the dramatic value of doublets, and that a climax may depend on a crinoline.

. . . the stage is not merely the meeting-place of all the arts, but is also the return of art to life.

Art has no other aim but her own perfection, and proceeds simply by her own laws . . .

The true dramatist . . . shows us life under the conditions of art, not art in the form of life.

The facts of art are diverse, but the essence of artistic effect is unity. Monarchy, Anarchy and Republicanism may contend for the government of nations; but a theatre should be in the power of a cultured despot. There may be division of labour, but there must be no division of mind . . . In fact, in art there is no special-ism, and a really artistic production should bear the impress of one master, and one master only, who not merely should design and arrange everything, but should have complete control over the way in which each dress is to be worn.

. . . our ordinary English novelists . . . fail . . . in concentration of style. Their characters are far too eloquent and talk themselves to tatters. What we want is a little more reality and a little less rhetoric . . . we wish that they would talk less and think more.

They lead us through a barren desert of verbiage to a mirage that they call life: we wander aimlessly through a very wilderness of words in search of one touch of nature. However, one should not be too severe on English novels; they are the only relaxation of the intellectually unemployed.

A poet can survive everything but a misprint.

. . . a poet without hysterics is rare.

In America the young are always ready to give to those who are older than themselves the full benefits of their inexperience . . . it may be truly said that no American child is ever blind to the deficiencies of its parents, no matter how much it may love them.

There is no such thing as a stupid American. Many Americans are horrid, vulgar, intrusive and impertinent, just as many English people are also; but stupidity is not one of the national vices. Indeed, in America there is no opening for a fool. They expect brains even from a boot-black, and get them.

As for marriage, it is one of their most popular institutions. The American man marries early, and the American woman marries often; and they get on extremely well together.

On the whole, the great success of marriage in the States is due partly to the fact that no American man is ever idle, and partly to the fact that no American wife is considered responsible for the quality of her husband's dinners.

America has never quite forgiven Europe for having been discovered somewhat earlier in history than itself.

. . . it would be a very good thing if people were taught how to speak. Language is the noblest instrument we have, either for the revealing or the concealing of thought; talk itself is a sort of spiritualized action; and conversation is one of the loveliest of the arts.

The only form of fiction in which real characters do not seem out of place is history.

Early in life she had discovered the important truth that nothing looks so like innocence as an indiscretion; and by a series of reckless escapades, half of them quite harmless, she had acquired all the privileges of a personality. She had more than once changed her husband; indeed, Debrett credits her with three marriages; but as she had never changed her lover, the world had long ago ceased to talk scandal about her.

Unless one is wealthy there is no use in being a charming fellow. Romance is the privilege of the rich, not the profession of the unemployed. The poor should be practical and prosaic. It is better to have a permanent income than to be fascinating.

Nobody, even in the provinces, should ever be allowed to ask an intelligent question about pure mathematics across a dinner table. A question of this kind is quite as bad as inquiring suddenly about the state of a man's soul . . .

Really domestic people are almost invariably bad talkers, as their very virtues in home life have dulled their interests in outer things. The very best mothers will insist on chattering of their babies, and prattling about infant education. In fact most women do not take sufficient interest in politics, just as most men are deficient in general reading. Still, anybody can be made to talk, except the very obstinate, and even a commercial traveller may be drawn out, and become quite interesting.

The health of a nation depends very largely on its mode of dress; the artistic feeling of a nation should find expression in its costume quite as much as in its architecture . . .

As a general rule, his verse is full of pretty echoes of other writers, but in one sonnet he makes a distinct attempt to be original and the result is extremely depressing.

> Earth wears her grandest robe, by autumn spun,
> *Like some stout matron who of youth has run*
> *The course, . . .*

is the most dreadful simile we have ever come across, even in poetry. Mr Griffiths should beware of originality. Like beauty, it is a fatal gift.

But what is the good of friendship if one cannot say exactly what one means? Anybody can say charming things and try to please and to flatter, but a true friend always says unpleasant things, and does not mind giving pain. Indeed, if he is a really true friend he prefers it, for he knows that then he is doing good.

The only thing that sustains one through life is the consciousness of the immense inferiority of everybody else, and this is a feeling that I have always cultivated.

I am so clever that sometimes I don't understand a single word of what I am saying.

I have always been of opinion that hard work is simply the refuge of people who have nothing whatever to do.

All that is known by that term [*fin de siècle*] I particularly admire and love. It is the fine flower of our civilization: the only thing that keeps the world from the commonplace, the coarse, the barbarous.

Flaubert did not write French prose, but the prose of a great artist who happened to be French.

I was thinking in bed this morning that the great superiority of France over England is that in France every bourgeois wants to be an artist, whereas in England every artist wants to be a bourgeois.

Prayer must never be answered: if it is, it ceases to be prayer and becomes correspondence.

I have made an important discovery . . . that alcohol, taken in sufficient quantities, produces all the effects of intoxication.

Missionaries, my dear! Don't you realize that missionaries are the divinely provided food for destitute and underfed cannibals? Whenever they are on the brink of starvation, Heaven in its infinite mercy sends them a nice plump missionary.

Philosophy teaches us to bear with equanimity the misfortunes of others.

As a rule the model, nowadays, is a pretty girl, from about twelve to twenty-five years of age, who knows nothing about art, cares less and is merely anxious to earn seven or eight shillings a day without much trouble. English models rarely look at a picture, and never venture on any aesthetic theories. In fact they realize very completely Mr Whistler's idea of the function of an art critic, for they pass no criticisms at all.

My own experience is that the more we study Art, the less we care for Nature . . . Art is our spirited protest, our gallant attempt to teach Nature her proper place.

Thinking is the most unhealthy thing in the world, and people die of it just as they die of any other disease. Fortunately, in England at any rate, thought is not catching.

Lying and poetry are arts – arts, as Plato saw, not unconnected with each other – and they require the most careful study, the most disinterested devotion.

M. Zola is determined to show that, if he has not got genius, he can at least be dull.

In literature we require distinction, charm, beauty and imaginative power. We don't want to be harrowed and disgusted with an account of the doings of the lower orders.

I quite admit that modern novels have many good points. All I insist on is that, as a class, they are quite unreadable.

George Meredith. His style is chaos illuminated by flashes of lightning. As a writer he has mastered everything except language: as a novelist he can do everything except tell a story: as an artist he is everything except articulate.

Art takes life as part of her rough material, recreates it and refashions it in fresh forms, is absolutely indifferent to fact, invents, imagines, dreams and keeps between herself and reality the impenetrable barrier of beautiful style, of decorative or ideal treatment.

Art itself is really a form of exaggeration; and selection, which is the very spirit of art, is nothing more than an intensified mode of over-emphasis.

The proper school to learn art in is not Life but Art.

Facts are not merely finding a footing-place in history, but they are usurping the domain of Fancy, and have invaded the kingdom of Romance. Their chilling touch is over everything. They are vulgarizing mankind.

Society sooner or later must return to its lost leader, the cultured and fascinating liar.

Life imitates Art far more than Art imitates Life . . . Life holds the mirror up to Art, and either reproduces some strange type imagined by painter or sculptor, or realizes in fact what has been dreamed in fiction.

For what is Nature? Nature is no great mother who has borne us. She is our creation. It is in our brain that she quickens to life. Things are because we see them, and what we see, and how we see it, depends on the Arts that have influenced us. To look at a thing is very different from seeing a thing. One does not see anything until one sees its beauty. Then, and then only, does it come into existence.

. . . imitation can be made the sincerest form of insult.

Yesterday evening Mrs Arundel insisted on my going to the window, and looking at the glorious sky, as she called it. Of course I had to look at it. She is one of those absurdly pretty Philistines to whom one can deny nothing. And what was it? It was simply a very second-rate Turner, a Turner of a bad period, with all the painter's worst faults exaggerated and over-emphasized.

The more abstract, the more ideal an art is, the more it reveals to us the temper of its age. If we wish to understand a nation by means of its art, let us look at its architecture or its music.

The fact is that we look back on the ages entirely through the medium of art, and art, very fortunately, has never once told us the truth.

To become a work of art is the object of living.

The English are always degrading truths into facts. When a truth becomes a fact it loses all its intellectual value.

There is a great deal to be said in favour of reading a novel backwards. The last page is as a rule the most interesting, and when one begins with the catastrophe or the *dénouement* one feels on pleasant terms of equality with the author. It is like going behind the scenes of a theatre. One is no longer taken in, and the hair-breadth escapes of the hero and the wild agonies of the heroine leave one absolutely unmoved. One knows the jealously guarded secret, and one can afford to smile at the quite unnecessary anxiety that the puppets of fiction always consider it their duty to display.

All charming people, I fancy, are spoiled. It is the secret of their attraction.

It is always a silly thing to give advice, but to give good advice is absolutely fatal. I hope you will never fall into that error. If you do, you will be sorry for it.

You forget that a thing is not necessarily true because a man dies for it.

Art, even the art of fullest scope and widest vision, can never really show us the external world. All that it shows us is our own soul, the one world of which we have any real cognizance . . . It is Art, and Art only, that reveals us to ourselves.

A critic should be taught to criticize a work of art without making any reference to the personality of the author. This, in fact, is the beginning of criticism.

Every great man nowadays has his disciples, and it is always Judas who writes the biography.

Learned conversation is either the affectation of the ignorant or the profession of the mentally unemployed.

Education is an admirable thing. But it is well to remember from time to time that nothing that is worth knowing can be taught.

Without the critical faculty, there is no artistic creation at all worthy of the name.

Anybody can write a three-volume novel. It merely requires a complete ignorance of both life and literature.

Anybody can make history. Only a great man can write it.

Self-denial is simply a method by which man arrests his progress, and self-sacrifice a survival of the mutilation of the savage . . .

The world is made by the singer for the dreamer.

It is sometimes said that the tragedy of an artist's life is that he cannot realize his ideal. But the true tragedy that dogs the steps of most artists is that they realize their ideal too absolutely. For, when the ideal is realized, it is robbed of its wonder and its mystery, and becomes simply a new starting-point for an ideal that is other than itself. This is the reason why music is the perfect type of art.

Conversation should touch everything, but should concentrate itself on nothing.

. . . life is terribly deficient in form. Its catastrophes happen in the wrong way and to the wrong people. There is a grotesque horror about its comedies, and its tragedies seem to culminate in farce. One is always wounded when one approaches it. Things last either too long or not long enough.

. . . all the arts are immoral, except those baser forms of sensual or didactic art that seek to excite to action of evil or of good. For action of every kind belongs to the sphere of ethics. The aim of art is simply to create a mood.

There is no country in the world so much in need of unpractical people as this country of ours. With us, Thought is degraded by its constant association with practice . . . We live in the age of the overworked, and the under-educated; the age in which people are so industrious that they become absolutely stupid.

The sure way of knowing nothing about life is to try to make oneself useful.

It is so easy for people to have sympathy with suffering. It is so difficult for them to have sympathy with thought.

An idea that is not dangerous is unworthy of being called an idea at all.

Man is least himself when he talks in his own person. Give him a mask, and he will tell you the truth.

For what is Truth? In matters of religion, it is simply the opinion that has survived. In matters of science, it is the ultimate sensation. In matters of art, it is one's last mood.

There are two ways of disliking art . . . One is to dislike it. The other, to like it rationally.

A little sincerity is a dangerous thing, and a great deal of it is absolutely fatal.

. . . there is much to be said in favour of modern journalism. By giving us the opinions of the uneducated, it keeps us in touch with the ignorance of the community.

To reveal art and conceal the artist is art's aim.

The critic is he who can translate into another manner or a new material his impression of beautiful things.

The highest, as the lowest, form of criticism is a mode of autobiography.

Those who find ugly meanings in beautiful things are corrupt without being charming. This is a fault.

Those who find beautiful meanings in beautiful things are the cultivated. For these there is hope.

There is no such thing as a moral or an immoral book. Books are well written, or badly written. That is all.

The moral life of man forms part of the subject-matter of the artist, but the morality of art consists in the perfect use of an imperfect medium. No artist desires to prove anything. Even things that are true can be proved.

Vice and virtue are to the artist materials for an art.

All art is at once surface and symbol.

Those who go beneath the surface do so at their peril.

Those who read the symbol do so at their peril.

It is the spectator, and not life, that art really mirrors.

When critics disagree the artist is in accord with himself.

We can forgive a man for making a useful thing as long as he does not admire it. The only excuse for making a useless thing is that one admires it intensely.

Experience was of no ethical value. It was merely the name men gave to their mistakes.

Women defend themselves by attacking, just as they attack by sudden and strange surrenders.

There is always something ridiculous about the emotions of people whom one has ceased to love.

There is a luxury in self-reproach. When we blame ourselves we feel that no one else has a right to blame us. It is the confession, not the priest, that gives us absolution.

Is insincerity such a terrible thing? I think not. It is merely a method by which we can multiply our personalities.

The critic has to educate the public; the artist has to educate the critic.

With the abolition of private property, then, we shall have true, beautiful, healthy Individualism. Nobody will waste his life in accumulating things, and the symbols for things. One will live. To live is the rarest thing in the world. Most people exist, that is all.

There is only one class in the community that thinks more about money than the rich, and that is the poor. The poor can think of nothing else. That is the misery of being poor.

High hopes were once formed of democracy; but democracy means simply the bludgeoning of the people by the people for the people.

The fact is, that civilization requires slaves. The Greeks were quite right there. Unless there are slaves to do the ugly, horrible, uninteresting work, culture and contemplation become almost impossible. Human slavery is wrong, insecure and demoralizing. On mechanical slavery, on the slavery of the machine, the future of the world depends.

A work of art is the unique result of a unique temperament . . . the moment that an artist takes notice of what other people want, and tries to supply the demand, he ceases to be an artist, and becomes a dull or an amusing craftsman, an honest or a dishonest tradesman.

Now Art should never try to be popular. The public should try to make itself artistic.

In England, the arts that have escaped best are the arts in which the public take no interest. Poetry is an instance of what I mean. We have been able to have fine poetry in England because the public do not read it, and consequently do not influence it.

In the old days men had the rack. Now they have the Press.

In England, Journalism, except in a few well-known instances, not having been carried to such excesses of brutality, is still a great factor, a really remarkable power. The tyranny that it proposes to exercise over people's private lives seems to me to be quite extraordinary. The fact is that the public have an insatiable curiosity to know everything, except what is worth knowing. Journalism, conscious of this, and having tradesman-like habits, supplies their demands. In centuries before ours the public nailed the ears of journalists to the pump. That was quite hideous. In this century journalists have nailed their own ears to the keyhole. That is much worse.

People sometimes inquire what form of government is most suitable for an artist to live under. To this question there is only one answer. The form of government that is most suitable to the artist is no government at all.

Anybody can sympathize with the sufferings of a friend, but it requires a very fine nature – it requires, in fact, that nature of a true Individualist – to sympathize with a friend's success.

Work is the curse of the drinking classes of this country.

Public opinion exists only where there are no ideas.

In old days books were written by men of letters and read by the public. Nowadays books are written by the public and read by nobody.

A subject that is beautiful in itself gives no suggestion to the artist. It lacks imperfection.

The only thing that the artist cannot see is the obvious. The only thing that the public can see is the obvious. The result is the Criticism of the Journalist.

Art is the only serious thing in the world. And the artist is the only person who is never serious.

Dandyism is the assertion of the absolute modernity of Beauty.

The only thing that can console one for being poor is extravagance. The only thing that can console one for being rich is economy.

One should never listen. To listen is a sign of indifference to one's hearers.

Even the disciple has his uses. He stands behind one's throne, and at the moment of one's triumph whispers in one's ear that, after all, one is immortal.

Those whom the gods love grow young.

The first duty in life is to be as artificial as possible. What the second duty is no one has as yet discovered.

Wickedness is a myth invented by good people to account for the curious attractiveness of others.

Those who see any difference between soul and body have neither.

A really well-made buttonhole is the only link between Art and Nature.

Religions die when they are proved to be true. Science is the record of dead religions.

The well-bred contradict other people. The wise contradict themselves.

Nothing that actually occurs is of the smallest importance.

Dullness is the coming of age of seriousness.

In all unimportant matters, style, not sincerity, is the essential. In all important matters, style, not sincerity, is the essential.

If one tells the truth, one is sure, sooner or later, to be found out.

Pleasure is the only thing one should live for. Nothing ages like happiness.

No crime is vulgar, but all vulgarity is crime. Vulgarity is the conduct of others.

Only the shallow know themselves.

Time is waste of money.

One should always be a little improbable.

There is a fatality about all good resolutions. They are invariably made too soon.

The only way to atone for being occasionally a little over-dressed is by being always absolutely over-educated.

To be premature is to be perfect.

Any preoccupation with ideas of what is right or wrong in conduct shows an arrested intellectual development.

Ambition is the last refuge of the failure.

A truth ceases to be true when more than one person believes in it.

In examinations the foolish ask questions that the wise cannot answer.

One should either be a work of art, or wear a work of art.

It is only the superficial qualities that last. Man's deeper nature is soon found out.

Industry is the root of all ugliness.

The ages live in history through their anachronisms.

The old believe everything: the middle-aged suspect everything: the young know everything.

The condition of perfection is idleness: the aim of perfection is youth.

Only the great masters of style ever succeed in being obscure.

To love oneself is the beginning of a life-long romance.

Oh, it is indeed a burning shame that there would be one law for men and another law for women. I think that there should be no law for anybody.

After the first glass, you see things as you wish they were. After the second, you see things as they are not. Finally you see things as they really are, and that is the most horrible thing in the world. (On absinthe)

My existence is a scandal.

It often happens that the real tragedies of life occur in such an inarticulate manner that they hurt one by their crude violence, their absolute incoherence, their absurd want of meaning, their entire lack of style.

The real fool . . . is he who does not know himself . . . The supreme vice is shallowness.

Nothing really at any period of my life was ever of the smallest importance to me compared with Art. But in the case of an artist, weakness is nothing less than a crime, when it is a weakness that paralyses the imagination.

The basis of character is will power . . .

Ultimately the bond of all companionship, whether in marriage or in friendship, is conversation . . .

Sins of the flesh are nothing. They are maladies for physicians to cure, if they should be cured. Sins of the soul alone are shameful.

The aim of love is to love: no more, and no less.

All homage is delightful to an artist and doubly sweet when youth brings it.

Prosperity, pleasure and success, may be rough of grain and common in fibre, but sorrow is the most sensitive of all created things. There is nothing that stirs in the whole world of thought to which sorrow does not vibrate in terrible and exquisite pulsation.

I was a man who stood in symbolic relations to the art and culture of my age . . . Few men hold such a position in their own lifetime, and have it so acknowledged.

To regret one's own experiences is to arrest one's own development. To deny one's own experiences is to put a lie into the lips of one's own life. It is no less than a denial of the soul.

What the artist is always looking for is the mode of existence in which soul and body are one and indivisible: in which the outward is expressive of the inward: in which form reveals.

Now it seems to me that love of some kind is the only possible explanation of the extraordinary amount of suffering that there is in the world.

Most people are other people. Their thoughts are someone else's opinions, their lives a mimicry, their passions a quotation.

Every single work of art is the fulfilment of a prophecy: for every work of art is the conversion of an idea into an image.

. . . all great ideas are dangerous.

Art only begins where Imitation ends . . .

All bad art is the result of good intentions.

By nature and by choice, I am extremely indolent.

I never put off till tomorrow what I can possibly do – the day after.

I am one of those who are made for exceptions, not for laws.

Praise makes me humble, but when I am abused I know I have touched the stars.

Where will it all end? Half the world does not believe in God, and the other half does not believe in me.

While the first editions of most classical authors are those coveted by bibliophiles, it is the second editions of my books that are the true rarities.

If I were all alone, marooned on some desert island and had my things with me, I should dress for dinner every evening.

I have the simplest tastes. I am always satisfied with the best.

A patriot put in prison for loving his country loves his country, and a poet in prison for loving boys loves boys. To have altered my life would have been to have admitted that Uranian love is ignoble. I hold it to be noble, more noble than other forms.

I entered prison with a heart of stone, thinking only of my pleasure, but now my heart has been broken; pity has entered my heart; I now understand that pity is the greatest and the most beautiful thing that there is in the world. And that's why I can't be angry with those who condemned me, nor with anyone, because then I would not have known all that.

I am not a scrap ashamed of having been in prison. I am horribly ashamed of the materialism of the life that brought me there. It was quite unworthy of an artist.

I love acting. It is so much more real than life.

As soon as people are old enough to know better, they don't know anything at all.

The tragedy of old age is not that one is old, but that one is young.

To get back my youth I would do anything in the world, except take exercise, get up early, or be respectable.

One can always be kind to people about whom one cares nothing.

Self-sacrifice is a thing that should be put down by law. It is so demoralizing to the people for whom one sacrifices oneself.

English people are far more interested in American barbarism than they are in American civilization.

We have really everything in common with America nowadays, except, of course, language.

America is the noisiest country that ever existed.

Bulk is their [Americans'] canon of beauty and size their standard of excellence.

The people of America understand money-making, but not how to spend it.

The American child educates its father and mother.

It is impossible not to think nobly of a country that has produced Patrick Henry, Thomas Jefferson, George Washington, and Jefferson Davis.

The American woman is the most decorated and decorative object I have seen in America.

For him [the American man] Art has no marvel, and Beauty no meaning, and the Past no message. He thinks that civilization began with the introduction of steam, and looks with contempt upon all centuries that had no hot-water apparatuses in their houses.

If the Americans are not the most well-dressed people in the world, they are the most comfortably dressed.

Every right article of apparel belongs equally to both sexes, and there is absolutely no such thing as a definitely feminine garment.

It is really only the idle classes who dress badly. Wherever physical labour of any kind is required, the costume used is, as a rule, absolutely right, for labour necessitates freedom, and without freedom there is no such thing as beauty in dress at all.

With an evening coat and a white tie, anybody, even a stockbroker, can gain a reputation for being civilized.

It is only shallow people who do not judge by appearances.

Being natural is simply a pose, and the most irritating pose I know.

Perhaps one never seems so much at one's ease as when one has to play a part.

I think a man should invent his own myth.

The meaning of any beautiful created thing is, at least, as much in the soul of him who looks at it, as it was in his soul who wrought it.

That is the mission of true art – to make us pause and look at a thing a second time.

The aim of art is no more to give pleasure than to give pain. The aim of art is to be art.

The public make use of the classics of a country as a means of checking the progress of Art. They degrade the classics into authorities. They use them as bludgeons for preventing the free expression of Beauty in new forms.

The best that one can say of most modern creative art is that it is just a little less vulgar than reality.

All art is quite useless.

The sign of a Philistine age is the cry of immorality against art.

Most of our modern portrait painters are doomed to absolute oblivion. They never paint what they see. They paint what the public sees, and the public never sees anything.

How can a man who regards success as a goal of life be a true artist?

No artist has ethical sympathies. An ethical sympathy in an artist is an unpardonable mannerism of style.

The young artist who paints nothing but beautiful things . . . misses one half of the world.

No great artist ever sees things as they really are. If he did, he would cease to be an artist.

The desire for beauty is merely a heightened form of the desire for life.

When the result is beautiful, the method is justified.

Beauty, like Wisdom, loves the lonely worshipper.

Those who do not love beauty more than truth never know the inmost shrine of art.

Devotion to beauty and to the creation of beautiful things is the test of all great civilized nations.

No object is so ugly that, under certain conditions of light and shade, or proximity to other things, it will not look beautiful; no object is so beautiful that, under certain conditions, it will not look ugly. I believe that in every twenty-four hours what is beautiful looks ugly, and what is ugly looks beautiful, once.

I have found that all ugly things are made by those who strive to make something beautiful, and that all beautiful things are made by those who strive to make something useful.

Utility will be always on the side of the beautiful things.

Good machinery is graceful . . . the line of strength and the line of beauty being one.

It is only by not paying one's bills that one can hope to live in the memory of the commercial classes.

Each class preaches the importance of those virtues it need not exercise. The rich harp on the value of thrift, the idle grow eloquent over the dignity of labour.

Extravagance is the luxury of the poor, penury the luxury of the rich.

We are often told that the poor are grateful for charity. Some of them are, no doubt, but the best amongst the poor are never grateful. They are ungrateful, discontented, disobedient, and rebellious. They are quite right to be so.

To recommend thrift to the poor is both grotesque and insulting. It is like advising a man who is starving to eat less.

Why should they [the poor] be grateful for the crumbs that fall from the rich man's table? They should be seated at the board, and are beginning to know it.

The real tragedy of the poor is that they can afford nothing but self-denial. Beautiful sins, like beautiful things, are the privilege of the rich.

The poor are wiser, more charitable, more kind, more sensitive than we are.

I quite sympathize with the rage of the English democracy against what they call the vices of the upper orders. The masses feel that drunkenness, stupidity, and immorality should be their own special property, and that if any one of us makes an ass of himself he is poaching on their preserves.

Those who have much are often greedy. Those who have little always share.

A *grande passion* is the privilege of people who have nothing to do. That is the one use of the idle classes of a country.

The inherited stupidity of the race – sound English common sense.

The growth of common sense in the English Church is a thing very much to be regretted.

Anybody can have common sense, provided that they have no imagination.

I love superstitions. They are the colour element of thought and imagination. They are the opponents of common sense.

Nowadays most people die of a sort of creeping common sense, and discover, when it is too late, that the only thing one never regrets are one's mistakes.

While to the claims of charity a man may yield and yet be free, to the claims of conformity no man may yield and remain free at all.

Selfishness is not living as one wishes to live, it is asking others to live as one wishes to live.

Conversation is one of the loveliest of the arts.

Recreation, not instruction, is the aim of conversation.

The maxim 'If you find the company dull, blame yourself' seems to us somewhat optimistic.

In the case of meeting a genius and a duke at dinner, the good talker will try to raise himself to the level of the former and to bring the latter down to his own level. To succeed among one's social superiors one must have no hesitation in contradicting them.

A man who can dominate a London dinner table can dominate the world.

I adore them [London dinner parties]. The clever people never listen, and the stupid people never talk.

It is only the intellectually lost who ever argue.

To believe is very dull. To doubt is intensely engrossing. To be on the alert is to live, to be lulled into security is to die.

I never approve, or disapprove, of anything now. It is an absurd attitude to take towards life. We are not sent into the world to air our moral prejudices.

The things one feels absolutely certain about are never true. That is the fatality of Faith, and the lesson of Romance.

No man dies for what he knows to be true. Men die for what they want to be true, for what some terror in their hearts tells them is not true.

Murder is always a mistake. One should never do anything that one cannot talk about after dinner.

There is no essential incongruity between crime and culture. We cannot re-write the whole of history for the purpose of gratifying our moral sense of what should be.

Starvation, and not sin, is the parent of modern crime.

A community is infinitely more brutalized by the habitual employment of punishment, than it is by the occasional occurrence of crime.

Prison life makes one see people and things as they really are. That is why it turns one to stone. It is the people outside who are deceived by the illusion of a life in constant motion.

To those who are in prison, tears are a part of every day's experience. A day in prison on which one does not weep is a day on which one's heart is hard, not a day on which one's heart is happy.

The most terrible thing about it [imprisonment] is not that it breaks one's heart – hearts are made to be broken – but that it turns one's heart to stone.

There has never been a creative age that has not been critical also.

The censure of the Puritan, whether real or affected, is always out of place in literary criticism, and shows a want of recognition of the essential distinction between art and life.

The moment criticism exercises any influence, it ceases to be criticism. The aim of the true critic is to try and chronicle his own moods, not to try to correct the masterpieces of others.

The true critic is he who bears within himself the dreams and ideas and feelings of myriad generations, and to whom no form of thought is alien, no emotional impulse obscure.

It is exactly because a man cannot do a thing that he is the proper judge of it.

Technique is really personality. That is the reason why the artist cannot teach it, why the pupil cannot learn it, and why the aesthetic critic can understand it.

It is only by intensifying his own personality that the critic can interpret the personality of others, and the more strongly this personality enters into the interpretation, the more real the interpretation becomes, the more satisfying, the more convincing, and the more true.

Astray: A Tale of a Country Town is a very serious volume. It has taken four people to write it, and even to read it requires assistance.

Andiatoroctè is the title of a volume of poems by the Rev. Clarence Walworth, of Albany, NY. It is a word borrowed from the Indians, and should, we think, be returned to them as soon as possible.

[On Guy de Maupassant:] He writes lurid little tragedies in which everybody is ridiculous; bitter comedies at which one cannot laugh for very tears.

Longfellow has no imitators, for of echoes themselves there are no echoes.

The one advantage of playing with fire . . . is that one never even gets singed. It is the people who don't know how to play with it who get burned up.

What is a cynic? A man who knows the price of everything and the value of nothing.

The sentimentalist is always a cynic at heart. Indeed sentimentality is merely the bank holiday of cynicism.

A sentimentalist is simply a man who desires to have the luxury of an emotion without paying for it.

He is a typical Englishman, always dull and usually violent.

A red-cheeked, white-whiskered creature who, like so many of his class, was under the impression that inordinate joviality can atone for an entire lack of ideas.

Like all people who try to exhaust a subject, he exhausted his listeners.

She behaves as if she was beautiful. Most American women do. It is the secret of their charm.

She was a curious woman, whose dresses always looked as if they had been designed in a rage and put on in a tempest.

She tried to look picturesque, but only succeeded in being untidy.

[She] talks more and says less than anybody I ever met. She is made to be a public speaker.

A dowdy dull girl, with one of those characteristic British faces, that, once seen, are never remembered.

Discontent is the first step in the progress of a man or a nation.

Disobedience, in the eyes of anyone who has read history, is man's original virtue. It is through disobedience that progress has been made, through disobedience and through rebellion.

In art, as in politics, there is but one origin for all revolutions, a desire on the part of man for a nobler form of life, for a freer method and opportunity of expression.

It is the first duty of a gentleman to dream.

A dreamer is one who can only find his way by moonlight, and his punishment is that he sees the dawn before the rest of the world.

Society often forgives the criminal; it never forgives the dreamer.

The one person who has more illusions than the dreamer is the man of action.

My duty to myself is to amuse myself terrifically.

People never think of cultivating a young girl's imagination. It is the great defect of modern education.

We teach people how to remember, we never teach them how to grow.

In the summer term Oxford teaches the exquisite art of idleness, one of the most important things that any University can teach.

I would have a workshop attached to every school, and one hour a day given up to the teaching of simple decorative arts. It would be a golden hour to the children.

A school should be the most beautiful place in every town and village – so beautiful that the punishment for undutiful children should be that they would be debarred from going to school the following day.

The secret of life is never to have an emotion that is unbecoming.

It is only shallow people who require years to get rid of an emotion. A man who is master of himself can end a sorrow as easily as he can invent a pleasure.

Beer, the Bible, and the seven deadly virtues have made our England what she is.

In England, a man who can't talk morality twice a week to a large, popular, immoral audience is quite over as a serious politician. There would be nothing left for him as a profession except Botany or the Church.

The English public always feels perfectly at its ease when a mediocrity is talking to it.

[The English] have a miraculous power of turning wine into water.

The English mind is always in a rage. The intellect of the race is wasted on the sordid and stupid quarrels of second-rate politicians or third-rate theologians.

A family is a terrible encumbrance, especially when one is not married.

Fashion is merely a form of ugliness so unbearable that we are compelled to alter it every six months.

An acquaintance that begins with a compliment is sure to develop into a real friendship. It starts in the right manner.

Laughter is not at all a bad beginning for a friendship, and it is far the best ending for one.

I always like to know everything about my new friends, and nothing about my old ones.

Formal courtesies will strain a close friendship.

Children begin by loving their parents. After a time they judge them. Rarely, if ever, do they forgive them.

San Francisco has the most lovely surroundings of any city except Naples.

California is an Italy without its art.

In no place is society more free and cordial and ready to give a friendly reception to a stranger than in California. In no part of the world is the individual more free from restraint.

This grey, monstrous London of ours, with its myriads of people, its sordid sinners, and its splendid sins.

We Irish are too poetical to be poets; we are a nation of brilliant failures, but we are the greatest talkers since the Greeks.

I don't like Switzerland: it has produced nothing but theologians and waiters.

There is this to be said in favour of the despot, that he, being an individual, may have culture, while the mob, being a monster, has none.

History never repeats itself. The historians repeat each other.

The one duty we owe to history is to re-write it.

Find expression for a sorrow, and it will become dear to you. Find expression for a joy, and you intensify its ecstasy.

The reason we all like to think so well of others is that we are all afraid for ourselves. The basis of optimism is sheer terror.

Laughter is the primeval attitude towards life – a mode of approach that survives only in artists and criminals.

Thought is wonderful, but adventure is more wonderful still.

While, in the opinion of society, Contemplation is the gravest thing of which any citizen can be guilty, in the opinion of the highest culture it is the proper occupation of man.

To do nothing at all is the most difficult thing in the world, the most difficult and the most intellectual.

Journalists record only what happens. What does it matter what happens? It is only the abiding things that are interesting, not the horrid incidents of everyday life.

Life is never fair.

Life goes faster than Realism, but Romanticism is always in front of Life.

The aim of life is self-development. To realize one's nature perfectly – that is what each of us is here for.

One can live for years sometimes without living at all, and then all life comes crowding into one single hour.

We can have in life but one great experience at best, and the secret of life is to reproduce that experience as often as possible.

Don't tell me that you have exhausted life. When a man says that one knows that life has exhausted him.

To become the spectator of one's own life is to escape the suffering of life.

Life cheats us with shadows. We ask it for pleasure. It gives it to us, with bitterness and disappointment in its train.

Literature always anticipates life. It does not copy it, but moulds it to its purpose. The nineteenth century, as we know it, is largely an invention of Balzac.

I hate vulgar realism in literature. The man who could call a spade a spade should be compelled to use one.

Are there not books that can make us live more in one single hour than life can make us live in a score of shameful years?

It was said of Trollope that he increased the number of our acquaintances without adding to our visiting list; but after reading the *Comédie Humaine* [by Balzac] one begins to believe that the only real people are the people who have never existed.

It is pleasanter to have the entrée to Balzac's society than to receive cards from all the duchesses in Mayfair.

To introduce real people into a novel or a play is a sign of an unimaginative mind, a coarse, untutored observation, and an entire absence of style.

The books that the world calls immoral books are books that show the world its own shame.

Schopenhauer has analysed the pessimism that characterizes modern thought, but Hamlet invented it.

No one survives being over-estimated, nor is there any surer way of destroying an author's reputation than to glorify him without judgement and to praise him without tact.

All love is a tragedy.

Misunderstanding . . . is the basis of love.

Those who are faithful know only the trivial side of love: it is the faithless who know love's tragedies.

Faithfulness is to the emotional life what consistency is to the life of the intellect – simply a confession of failure.

Lust . . . makes one love all that one loathes.

It is difficult not to be unjust to what one loves.

One should always be in love. That is the reason one should never marry.

The proper basis for marriage is a mutual misunderstanding.

Married life is merely a habit, a bad habit.

How marriage ruins a man! It's as demoralizing as cigarettes, and far more expensive.

The happiness of a married man . . . depends on the people he has not married.

The one charm of marriage is that it makes a life of deception absolutely necessary for both parties.

The world has grown so suspicious of anything that looks like a happy married life.

It's most dangerous nowadays for a husband to pay attention to his wife in public. It always makes people think he beats her when they are alone.

Nowadays everybody is jealous of everyone else, except, of course, husband and wife.

Twenty years of romance make a woman look like a ruin; but twenty years of marriage make her something like a public building.

Girls never marry the men they flirt with. Girls don't think it right.

Men marry because they are tired; women because they are curious. Both are disappointed.

Men know life too early . . . Women know life too late. That is the difference between men and women.

The only way a woman can ever reform a man is by boring him so completely that he loses all possible interest in life.

When a man has once loved a woman, he will do anything for her, except continue to love her.

A man can be happy with any woman, as long as he does not love her.

Men always want to be a woman's first love. That is their clumsy vanity . . . Women have a more subtle instinct about things. What [they] like is to be a man's last romance.

There is only one real tragedy in a woman's life. The fact that the past is always her lover, and her future invariably her husband.

Between men and women there is no friendship possible. There is passion, enmity, worship, love, but no friendship.

Women have a wonderful instinct about things. They can discover everything except the obvious.

One should never trust a woman who tells one her real age. A woman who would tell one that, would tell one anything.

It is only very ugly or very beautiful women who ever hide their faces.

If a woman wants to hold a man she has merely to appeal to what is worst in him.

I never travel without my diary. One should always have something sensational to read in the train.

Between the famous and the infamous there is but one step, if so much as one.

Formerly we used to canonize our great men; nowadays we vulgarize them.

Nothing looks so like innocence as an indiscretion.

There are many things that we would throw away if we were not afraid that others might pick them up.

Why is it that one runs to one's ruin? Why has destruction such a fascination?

One needs misfortunes to live happily.

To live in happiness, you must know some unhappiness in life.

The happy people of the world have their value, but only the negative value of foils. They throw up and emphasize the beauty and the fascination of the unhappy.

What fire does not destroy, it hardens.

Suffering and the community of suffering makes people kind.

While to propose to be a better man is a piece of unscientific cant, to have become a *deeper* man is the privilege of those who have suffered.

There is no truth comparable to Sorrow. There are times when Sorrow seems to me to be the only truth.

Sorrow, being the supreme emotion of which man is capable, is at once the type and test of all great Art.

All excess, as well as all renunciation, brings its own punishment.

Nothing succeeds like excess.

Pure modernity of form is always somewhat vulgarizing.

Nothing is so dangerous as being too modern; one is apt to grow old-fashioned quite suddenly.

The value of the telephone is the value of what two people have to say.

Why does not science, instead of troubling itself about sunspots, which nobody ever saw, or, if they did, ought not to speak about; why does not science busy itself with drainage and sanitary engineering? Why does it not clean the streets and free the rivers from pollution?

Only one thing remains infinitely fascinating to me, the mystery of moods. To be master of these moods is exquisite, to be mastered by them more exquisite still.

You people who go in for being consistent have just as many moods as others have. The only difference is that your moods are rather meaningless.

There must be no mood with which one cannot sympathize, no dead mode of life that one cannot make alive.

Morality is simply the attitude we adopt towards people whom we personally dislike.

There is no such thing as morality, for there is no general rule of spiritual health; it is all personal, individual.

Science is out of the reach of morals, for her eyes are fixed upon eternal truths. Art is out of the reach of morals, for her eyes are fixed upon things beautiful and immortal and ever-changing. To morals belong the lower and less intellectual spheres.

Modern morality consists in accepting the standard of one's age. I consider that for any man of culture to accept the standard of his age is a form of the grossest immorality.

Manners are of more importance than morals.

The moral is too obvious.

I never came across anyone in whom the moral sense was dominant who was not heartless, cruel, vindictive, log-stupid, and entirely lacking in the smallest sense of humanity. Moral people, as they are termed, are simple beasts.

In old days . . . to be a bit better than one's neighbour was considered excessively vulgar and middle-class. Nowadays, with our modern mania for morality, everyone has to pose as a paragon of purity, incorruptibility, and all the other seven deadly virtues.

[Al]though of all poses a moral pose is the most offensive, still to have a pose at all is something.

Music is the art . . . which most completely realizes the artistic idea, and is the condition to which all the other arts are constantly aspiring.

Music . . . creates for one a past of which one has been ignorant, and fills one with a sense of sorrows that have been hidden from one's tears.

If one plays good music, people don't listen, and if one plays bad music, people don't talk.

I like Wagner's music better than anybody's. It is so loud that one can talk the whole time without people hearing what one says.

Musical people are so absurdly unreasonable. They always want one to be perfectly dumb at the very moment when one is longing to be absolutely deaf.

The things of nature do not really belong to us; we should leave them to our children as we have received them.

In nature there is, for me at any rate, healing power.

We all look at Nature too much, and live with her too little.

If Nature had been comfortable, mankind would never have invented architecture.

Nature, which makes nothing durable, always repeats itself so that nothing which it makes may be lost.

Nature is always behind the age.

Whenever we have returned to Life and Nature, our work has always become vulgar, common, and uninteresting.

Only dull people are brilliant at breakfast.

There are only two kinds of people who are really fascinating – people who know absolutely everything, and people who know absolutely nothing.

Of course I plagiarize. It is the privilege of the appreciative man.

It is only the unimaginative who ever invent. The true artist is known by the use he makes of what he annexes, and he annexes everything.

True originality is to be found rather in the use made of a model than in the rejection of all models . . . we should not quarrel with the reed if it whispers to us the music of the lyre.

Every word in a play has a musical as well as an intellectual value, and must be made expressive of a certain emotion.

The tears that we shed at a play are a type of the exquisite sterile emotion that it is the function of Art to awaken. We weep, but we are not wounded. We grieve, but our grief is not bitter.

I never write plays for anyone. I write plays to amuse myself. After, if people want to act in them, I sometimes allow them to do so.

There are two ways of disliking my plays. One is to dislike them, the other is to like *Earnest*.

Pleasure is Nature's test, her sign of approval. When man is happy he is in harmony with himself and his environment.

No civilized man ever regrets a pleasure, and no uncivilized man ever knows what a pleasure is.

I adore simple pleasures. They are the last refuge of the complex.

A cigarette is the perfect type of a perfect pleasure. It is exquisite, and it leaves one unsatisfied. What more can one want?

I don't regret for a single moment having lived for pleasure. I did it to the full, as one should do everything that one does to the full. There was no pleasure I did not experience.

I like persons better than principles, and I like persons with no principles better than anything else in the world.

I don't like principles . . . I prefer prejudices.

It is personalities, not principles, that move the age.

The public is wonderfully tolerant. It forgives everything except genius.

The public is largely influenced by the *look* of a book. So are we all. It is the only artistic thing about the public.

Public Opinion . . . is an attempt to organize the ignorance of the community.

Public opinion exists only where there are no ideas.

I am very fond of the public, and, personally, I always patronize the public very much.

He never touches water: it goes to his head at once.

There are a hundred things I want not to say to you.

I can stand brute force, but brute reason is quite unbearable. There is something unfair about its use. It is hitting below the intellect.

Science can never grapple with the irrational. That is why it has no future before it.

I wonder who it was defined man as a rational animal. It was the most premature definition ever given. Man is many things, but he is not rational.

One is tempted to define man as a rational animal who always loses his temper when he is called upon to act in accordance with the dictates of reason.

Relations are simply a tedious pack of people, who haven't got the remotest knowledge of how to live, nor the smallest instinct about when to die.

Relations never lend one any money, and won't give one credit, even for genius. They are a sort of aggravated form of the public.

I can't help detesting my relations. I suppose it comes from the fact that none of us can stand other people having the same faults as ourselves.

After a good dinner one can forgive anybody, even one's own relations.

I have never heard any man mention his brother. The subject seems distasteful to most men.

When one is in love one always begins by deceiving oneself and one always ends by deceiving others. That is what the world calls a romance.

The worst of having a romance is that it leaves one so unromantic.

There is no such thing as a romantic experience; there are romantic memories, and there is the desire for romance – that is all. Our most fiery moments of ecstasy are merely shadows of what somewhere else we have felt, or of what we long some day to feel.

It is very romantic to be in love, but there is nothing romantic about a definite proposal. Why, one may be accepted. One usually is, I believe. Then the excitement is all over.

The very essence of romance is uncertainty. If I ever get married, I'll certainly try to forget the fact.

Lovers are happiest when they are in doubt.

The romance of life is that one can love so many people and marry but one.

Women . . . spoil every romance by trying to make it last forever.

Every romance that one has in one's life is a romance lost to one's art.

How silly to write on pink paper! It looks like the beginning of a middle-class romance.

Romance is the privilege of the rich, not the profession of the unemployed.

The best style is that which seems an unconscious result rather than a conscious aim.

Style largely depends on the way the chin is worn.

Sentiment is all very well for the buttonhole. But the essential thing for a necktie is style. A well-tied tie is the first serious step in life.

In the mode of the knotting of one's necktie or the conduct of one's cane there is an entire creed of life.

In matters of grave importance, style, not sincerity, is the vital thing.

Success is a science; if you have the conditions, you get the result.

There is something about success, actual success, that is a little unscrupulous, something about ambition that is unscrupulous always.

There is something vulgar in all success. The greatest men fail – or seem to the world to have failed.

Actions are the first tragedy in life, words are the second. Words are perhaps the worst. Words are merciless.

There is no mode of action, no form of emotion, that we do not share with the lower animals. It is only by language that we rise above them, or above each other – by language, which is the parent, and not the child of thought.

Lots of people act well . . . but very few people talk well, which shows that talking is much more the difficult thing of the two, and much the finer thing also.

It is very much more difficult to talk about a thing than to do it.

Whenever people talk to me about the weather, I always feel certain that they mean something else.

It is much cleverer to talk nonsense than to listen to it . . . and a much rarer thing too, in spite of all the public may say.

I can resist everything except temptation.

The only way to get rid of a temptation is to yield to it. Resist it, and your soul grows sick with longing for the things it has forbidden to itself.

There are terrible temptations that it requires strength, strength and courage, to yield to. To stake all one's life on one throw – whether the stakes be power or pleasure, I care not – there is no weakness in that. There is a horrible, a terrible courage.

Life's aim, if it has one, is simply to be always looking for temptations. There are not nearly enough. I sometimes pass a whole day without coming across a single one.

One can only write in cities.

When one is in town one amuses oneself. When one is in the country one amuses other people. It is excessively boring.

Anybody can be good in the country. There are no temptations there.

It is pure, unadulterated country life. They get up early because they have so much to do, and go to bed early because they have so little to think about.

I don't think any one at all morally responsible for what he or she does at an English country house.

Truth is entirely and absolutely a matter of style.

The truth is rarely pure and never simple.

To lie finely is an art, to tell the truth is to act according to nature.

The aim of the liar is simply to charm, to delight, to give pleasure. He is the very basis of civilized society.

Society sooner or later must return to its lost leader, the cultured and fascinating liar.

If a man is sufficiently unimaginative to produce evidence in support of a lie, he might just as well speak the truth at once.

It is curious how vanity helps the successful man and wrecks the failure.

Egotism is not without its attractions. When people talk to us about others they are usually dull. When they talk to us about themselves they are nearly always interesting.

Humility is for the hypocrite, modesty for the incompetent.

Conceit is the privilege of the creative.

It would be unfair to expect other people to be as remarkable as oneself.